How many words can you think of that have an oy sound?
Here are a few to get you started:

Toy

Boy

Do long trips in a car annoy you? If they do, you might enjoy a trip on a train.

Trains are quick. A trip on a train will not be as long as a trip in a car.

You need a ticket to get on a train. You can get one from an employee at a booth.

Then, you need to wait at a platform. You will see the train come in along the track.

Track

Platform

When you get on a train, you might hear a person on the speaker. This is the conductor.

The conductor will tell people what stop the train is at and what the next one will be.

If you need to travel far, you can get a high-speed train. This will help a long trip seem fast.

Some people collect toy trains from different years. They might be mini, but they can still run on a track.

Some trains are just for crops, such as grain, corn and soy. Some are for coal and oil.

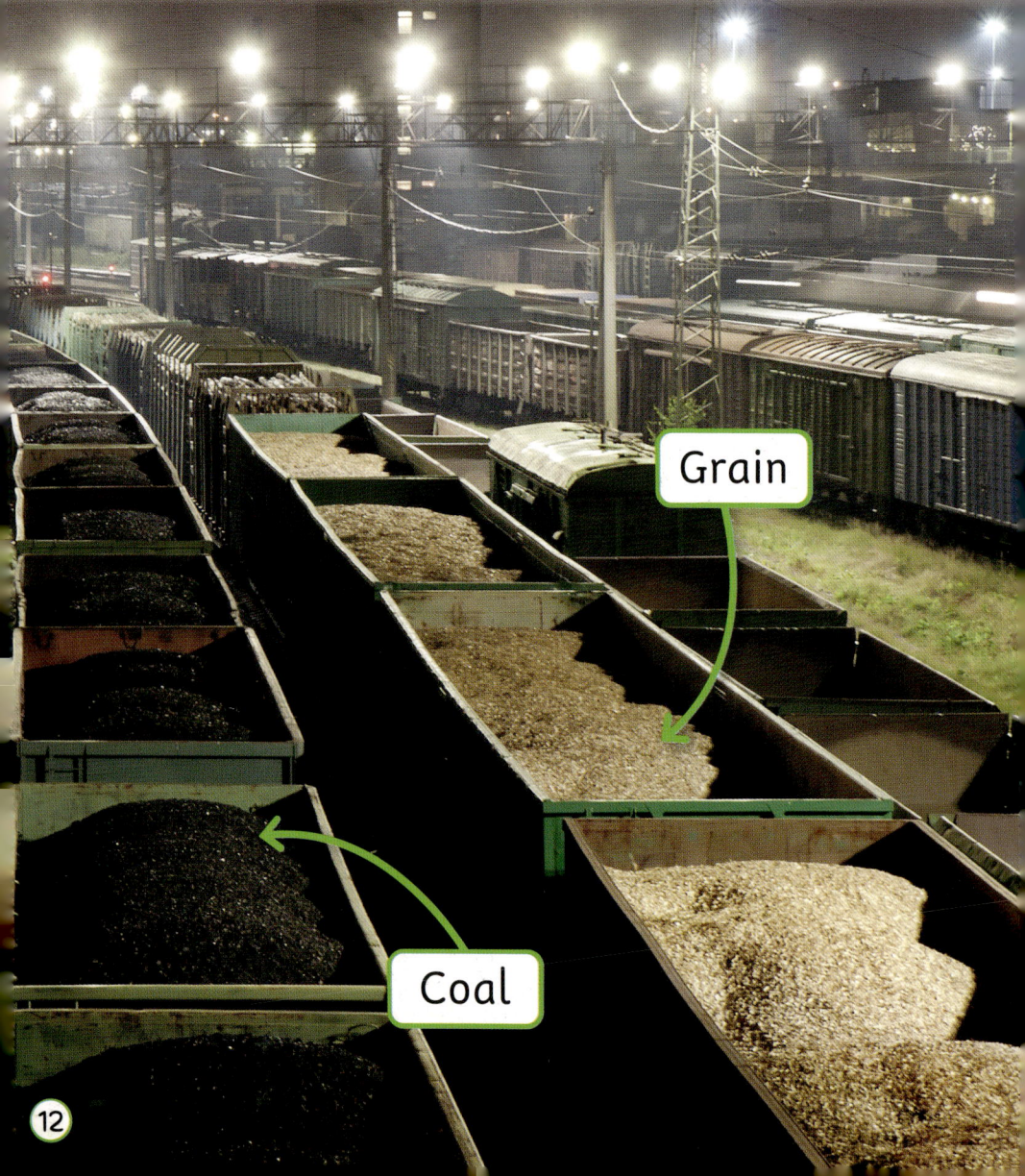

Grain

Coal

Trains like this are important. They help transport lots of the things you get from the shops.

Until we had modern trains, we had steam trains. These trains burned coal to get them to go.

Steam
train

Modern trains do not puff as much as steam trains!

BookLife PUBLISHING

BookLife Readers

©2023 **BookLife Publishing Ltd.**
King's Lynn, Norfolk, PE30 4LS, UK.

ISBN 978-1-80505-061-2

All rights reserved. Printed in China.
A catalogue record for this book is
available from the British Library.

Trains
Written by Charis Mather
Designed by Jasmine Pointer

An Introduction to BookLife Readers...

Our Readers have been specifically created in line with the London Institute of Education's approach to book banding and are phonetically decodable and ordered to support each phase of the Letters and Sounds document.

Each book has been created to provide the best possible reading and learning experience. Our aim is to share our love of books with children, providing both emerging readers and prolific page-turners with beautiful books that are guaranteed to provoke interest and learning, regardless of ability.

BOOK BAND GRADED using the Institute of Education's approach to levelling.

PHONETICALLY DECODABLE supporting each phase of Letters and Sounds.

EXERCISES AND QUESTIONS to offer reinforcement and to ascertain comprehension.

CLEAR DESIGN to inspire and provoke engagement, providing the reader with clear visual representations of each non-fiction topic.

AUTHOR INSIGHT:
CHARIS MATHER

Charis Mather is a children's author at BookLife Publishing who has a love for reading and writing. Her studies in linguistics and experiences working with young readers have given her a knack for writing material that suits a range of ages and skill levels. Charis is passionate about producing books that emphasise the fun in reading and is convinced that no matter how much you already know, there is always something new to learn.

PHASE 5
/oy/

This book focuses on /oy/ and is a Green level 5 book band.

Image Credits Images are courtesy of Shutterstock.com. With thanks to Getty Images, Thinkstock Photo and iStockphoto. Cover – Oleksiy Mark, Kevin_Hsieh, MIKHAIL GRACHIKOV. 2–3 – Pixel-Shot, Billion Photos. 4–5 – Artens, Ceri Breeze. 6–7 – ShutterStockStudio, olgaarmawir. 8–9 – Savvapanf Photo, BlueOrange Studio. 10–11 – pedrosala, Ian Fox. 12–13 – Funnycreature, Azovsky. 14–15 – www.Foto-Format.com, Mgr. Nobody.